Why I Love...

By Alex Samtani
7 years old

To order additional copies of this book, contact:
Xlibris
UK TFN: 0800 0148620 (Toll Free inside the UK)
UK Local: 02 0369 56328 (+44 20 3695 6328 from outside the UK)
www.xlibrispublishing.co.uk
Orders@ Xlibrispublishing.co.uk

ISBN: Softcover   978-1-6698-9025-6
         EBook   978-1-6698-9024-9

Library of Congress Control Number: 2023913933

Print information available on the last page

Rev. date: 07/28/2023

Why I Love...

Why I love my dad..............

He looks after me.
He plays football with me.
He looks like Pep Guardiola who coaches my favourite football team Manchester City.

Why I love my mummy.....

She is beautiful, kind and loves me very much.
She hugs me and says she is proud of me.
She wants me to do well in school.
She is an engineer.

Why I love football...........

It is the best thing in the world.
It makes me feel happy and it is very exciting.
I want to be a footballer when I grow up.
My favourite team is Manchester City.

Why I love my friends...........

I have many friends.
We have so much fun.
We are happy together.
We laugh a lot.
We play nice games.
Our imagination is unbelievable.
Sometimes we are naughty.

Why I love my baby sitter Didi..............

She looks after me when my mummy and daddy are at work.
She makes delicious food.
She takes me on the bus, to the park and to swimming.
Sometimes I meet my friends with their babysitters at the park.

Why I love maths.............

Numbers are very cool.
I enjoy doing different sums with numbers.
Maths is my favourite subject.
I won the Time Table Rock Stars competition at my school.
My dad is good at maths and I want to be like my dad.

Why I love science...........

I can do experiments, some are messy.
I learn how things are made and how they work.
I like facts and science has many facts.
I want to invent something.

Why I love my teachers...........

I go to a very nice school near to Kew Gardens.
My teachers share so much knowledge with my
friends and me.
They look after us and tell us interesting stories.
The head teacher is very kind.

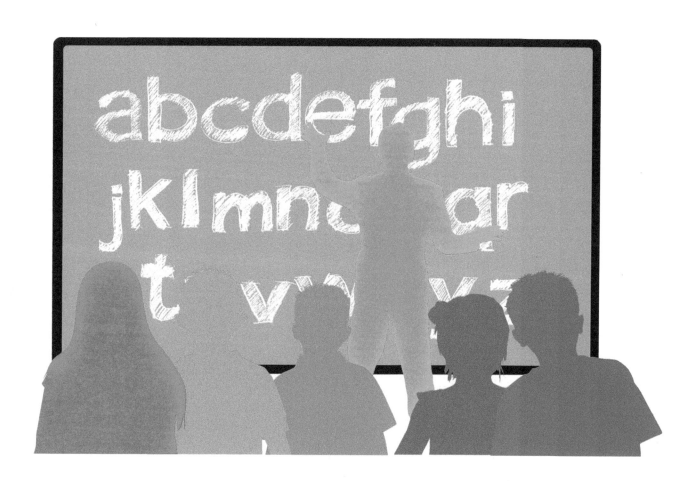

Why I love my grandparents.....

I have two grandparents.
They live in the Caribbean where it is always sunny and hot.
They give me many hugs, gifts and tasty fruits to eat.
They say nice things about me.

Why I love planes...........

Planes take me to far away lands where I can have adventures.
I like being high up in the sky, seeing the beautiful clouds and feeling the bumpy turbulence.
My mum does not like turbulence.
Sometimes I imagine the clouds are different items or animals.

Why I love summer.....

Sunshine makes me smile.
I can run outdoors without a coat when it's hot
so I go faster.
I can go swimming.
I get long school holidays in summer.

Milton Keynes UK
Ingram Content Group UK Ltd.
UKHW051204040923
428010UK00008B/37